D1097467

DISCOVERY PACK

AMAZING SCIENCE
EXPERIMENTS

ANNA CLAYBOURNE

ARCTURUS

This edition published in 2019 by Arcturus Publishing Limited
26/27 Bickels Yard, 151–153 Bermondsey Street,
London SE1 3HA

Copyright © Arcturus Holdings Limited

All rights reserved. No part of this publication may be reproduced,
stored in a retrieval system, or transmitted, in any form or by any means,
electronic, mechanical, photocopying, recording or otherwise, without
prior written permission in accordance with the provisions of the
Copyright Act 1956 (as amended). Any person or persons who do any
unauthorised act in relation to this publication may be liable to criminal
prosecution and civil claims for damages.

Author: Anna Claybourne
Science consultant: Thomas Canavan
Experiment illustrations: Jessica Secheret
Other illustrations: Richard Watson
Photos: Shutterstock
Design: Supriya Sahai

ISBN: 978-1-78888-717-5

CH006775US
Supplier 13, Date 0119, Print run 7754

Printed in China

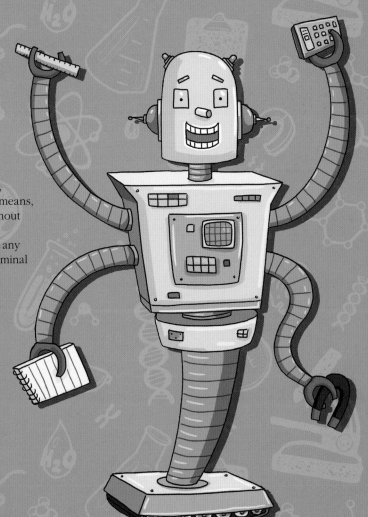

CONTENTS

This pack contains a poster and sticker sheet.
To complete the poster artwork, you should
place stickers over the silhouettes. Make
sure that the shapes match! There are extra
stickers, too, just for fun.

START EXPERIMENTING!

This book is packed with exciting experiments that go bang, make a big splat, or are so incredible you won't believe your eyes! But there's nothing magical in these pages—it's all real-life amazing **SCIENCE**.

WHAT YOU'LL NEED

You can do most of these experiments with everyday items you'll find around the house, or can buy easily and cheaply at a supermarket or hardware store.

Some useful things to have handy are ...

* Paper and cardboard
* Pens and pencils
* String
* Glue
* Tape
* Straws (plastic ones are best)
* Plates, bowls, jugs, and plastic food containers
* Scissors
* Paper cups
* Balloons

STAY SAFE!

Experiments are fun, but some of them can be dangerous if they're not done carefully … so don't forget these safety tips:

✸ You will need an adult to help with experiments that involve cooking and heating, matches and candles, and sharp cutting tools. Wherever an experiment has something like this in it, you'll see this sign to remind you:

⚠ **ASK AN ADULT!**

✸ Follow all the instructions carefully to make sure you use all the equipment and materials in a safe way.

✸ Stand back from anything that's moving fast, or that involves eruptions or explosions. And don't throw, shoot, or whirl things around unless you're completely sure there's no one nearby.

And remember...

Always do experiments somewhere that's easy to clean up, like a kitchen or bathroom—NOT on the fancy carpet! And make sure you do clean up after yourself. Some of these experiments are messy!

So, are you ready to see some science?
Step this way …

NOISY EXPERIMENTS

These experiments make loud bangs, weird noises, or cool music, to help you find out what sound really is, and how it works.

What is sound?
Basically, we hear sound when things move and vibrate, or shake quickly to and fro. These movements make the air vibrate, too. The vibrations spread out through the air and reach our ears.

Sound waves
When you drop an object into liquid it makes the water move, and ripples spread out in a circle until they touch the edge. Sound is the same, but instead of spreading out in a flat layer, the sound waves go in all directions.

Moving & shaking

For example, if someone hits a cymbal, the metal vibrates, and that makes invisible ripples, or sound waves, spread out in the air all around it. You hear the sound when the sound waves reach your ears.

Make a noise!

There are lots of ways to make a sound by getting something to vibrate. Try this simple experiment with a balloon:

1. Blow up a balloon, but don't tie it closed.

2. Hold the sides of the opening of the balloon, and pull them away from each other.

3. Slowly let the air out of the balloon. Try stretching the opening tightly and less tightly as the air escapes to see if you can change the sound.

HOW DOES IT WORK?

As the air pushes through the narrow gap in the opening, it makes the rubbery balloon skin vibrate. This makes a loud squeaking sound.

Watch it

Sound vibrations are often so small or so fast that they can be hard to see clearly. But in this case, you should be able to see the neck of the balloon vibrating in a blur.

7

GLITTER DISCO

This experiment will let you see the vibrations that sounds make—and get some glitter to dance!

WHAT YOU'LL NEED:

* A large radio with a speaker on the front, or a hi-fi speaker
* Glitter flakes (not the powdery kind—larger flakes work better)
* A large plastic plate or round tray
* Plastic wrap (sometimes called clingfilm)

1. Tear off a large piece of plastic wrap and stretch it over the plate so that it's as flat and smooth as possible. Tuck the plastic wrap under the plate to hold it in place.

2. Get your radio or speaker, and lie it down so that the speaker part is facing upward. You may have to ask someone to hold it steady.

3. Put your plastic wrap-covered plate right over the middle of the speaker. If you can see two speaker openings, use the bigger one if there is one.

4. Shake a small amount of glitter onto the middle of the plastic wrap—about a teaspoonful. (Be careful not to spill glitter into the speaker.)

5. Play some music—something with a clear beat, like rock, disco, or dance music—and turn it up loud (or as loud as you're allowed!).

HOW DOES IT WORK?

When the speaker makes sound, the sound makes vibrations in the air. They pass through the plate into the plastic wrap, making it vibrate up and down. Louder sounds make bigger vibrations! This makes the glitter jump in the air and move in time to the music.

Want to try making something else dance—or don't have any glitter? Lots of other things work well. Try small sequins, flaky sea salt, or small seeds, like caraway or sesame seeds.

STRAW TROMBONE

If you have a real trombone and know how to play it, you'll definitely be able to make a racket. But if not, here's the next best thing—a working trombone made out of household items!

WHAT YOU'LL NEED:

* Two straws, one slightly wider than the other
* A piece of thin cardboard at least 6 x 6 inches (15 x 15cm)
* A pencil
* Scissors
* Clear tape

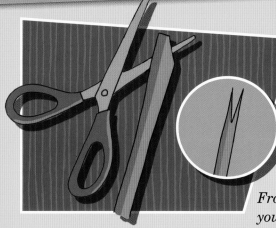

From the side, your straw should look like this.

1. Take the narrower straw, and flatten one end of it between your fingers. Then use the scissors to carefully snip off the sides to form a point.

2. Press the end again until it's as flat as you can make it. Then test it to see if it makes a sound. Put the cut end of the straw about 1 inch (3cm) inside in your mouth, and blow hard. If there's no sound, press the end flat again.

3. Copy this shape onto the cardboard, making it about 6 inches (15cm) across, and cut it out. Curve it into a cone, with a straw-sized hole at the top, and tape in place. Stick one end of the wider straw into the cone, and tape together.

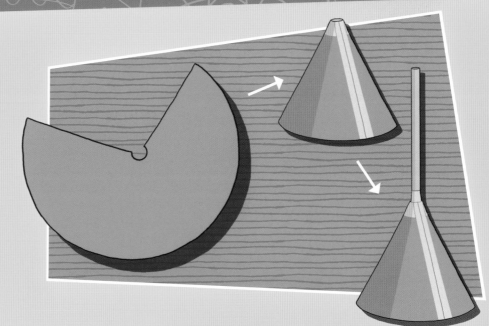

4. Now slide the wider straw over the narrower straw, so that it can slide up and down. Your trombone is ready to play!

HOW DOES IT WORK?

When you blow into the straw, your breath makes the pieces at the cut end vibrate, and this makes a noise. The air inside the straws vibrates, too. The longer the tube, the more space the air has to vibrate, and the lower the sound will be. The cone, or "bell," on the end of the trombone helps to make the sound louder.

Can you use the sliding movement to make higher and lower notes? This will work best if the straws are only slightly different sizes and fit together tightly.

SCI-FI SOUNDS

With nothing more than a metal spring toy and a paper cup, you can make a sound like a sci-fi spaceship zapping an alien enemy with a laser gun. Try it and see!

WHAT YOU'LL NEED:
* A metal spring toy, the type that "walks" down stairs
* A paper cup
* Clear tape
* Pointy scissors or a craft knife
* A metal spoon or fork

① ASK AN ADULT!

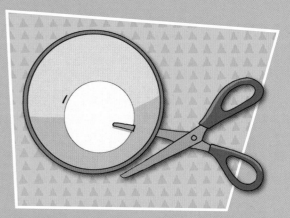

1. Ask an adult to cut two small, horizontal slots near the bottom of the cup, using the scissors or knife. They should be right next to the base of the cup, just above it.

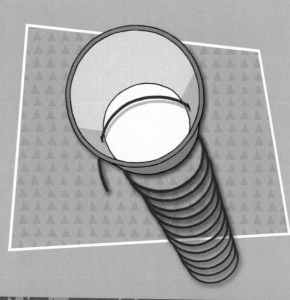

2. Now take the end of the spring toy and carefully slide it through both the slots, so that the first part of the spring lies flat against the cup base.

3. Hold the cup up in the air, so that the spring toy dangles down, almost touching the floor. (You might need to stand on a chair for this.)

HOW DOES IT WORK?

The space-age sound is created by lots of vibrations moving up the spring from the ground. The faster vibrations make higher-pitched sounds, which reach the cup first, followed by the lower ones. This makes the metallic "Pneeeeow!" noise that sounds like a space weapon.

To make the sound louder, tape a piece of cardboard around the cup in a cone shape to act as a megaphone.

4. To make the ray gun effect, make the spring toy bounce off the floor. The sound will come out of the cup. You can also try hitting the spring with the spoon.

BOTTLE BAGPIPE

This bizarre instrument makes a noise a bit like a bagpipe—or maybe a buzzing fly, or a ship's foghorn. See what you think it sounds like!

WHAT YOU'LL NEED:

* A small or medium-sized drinks bottle made of tough plastic
* A balloon
* Pointy scissors
* A straw
* Clear tape
* Paper

⚠ ASK AN ADULT!

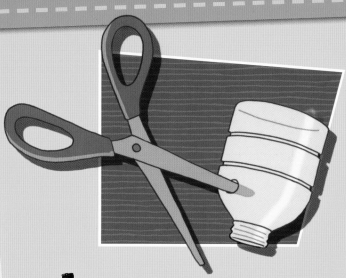

1.

Ask an adult to cut the top off the bottle as neatly as possible. Then ask them to make a small hole in the side of the bottle, the same size as the straw, by sticking the pointy tip of the scissors into the plastic and twisting it around.

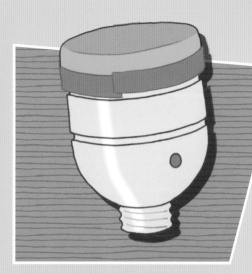

2.

Next, cut the open end off the balloon and stretch it as tightly as you can over the open end of the bottle. When it's as tight and flat as you can get it, fix the edge to the bottle with sticky tape.

3.

Roll a piece of paper into a tight tube and stick it through the neck of the bottle, so that it presses against the balloon. Let it go so that it unrolls itself slightly and fits tightly into the bottle neck.

4.

Now stick the straw through the hole in the bottle.

5.

Hold the bottle in one hand and the paper tube in the other. Pushing the paper tube gently against the balloon, blow hard into the straw.

HOW DOES IT WORK?

When you blow air into the bottle, it pushes against the balloon and makes it vibrate. The vibrations spread into the paper tube, too, making a noise that comes out of the end of the tube.

SMARTPHONE SPEAKERS

These fantastic speakers will turn the tinny sound of a smartphone into a homemade boombox. All you need are some paper cups and a kitchen roll tube.

WHAT YOU'LL NEED:

* The tube from the inside of a kitchen roll
* 2 paper cups
* A pencil
* Pointy scissors
* A smartphone with music stored on it

⚠ ASK AN ADULT!

If you don't have a kitchen roll tube, you can use part of a poster tube, or the cardboard tube from inside a roll of wrapping paper. Ask an adult to cut it to about 10 inches (25cm) long.

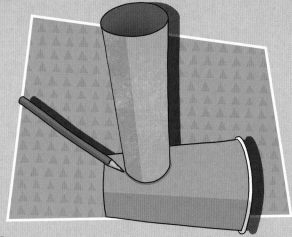

1. Hold the end of the tube against the side of one of the cups, close to the bottom. Draw around the tube with the pencil to make a circle.

2. Cut out the circle, with an adult's help, cutting very slightly inside the line you have drawn. Then do the same thing with the other cup.

3. Hold the end of your smartphone against the middle of the tube, and draw around it with the pencil. Ask an adult to help you cut out the shape, cutting just inside the line.

4. Now push the ends of the tube into the holes in the paper cups, as far as they will go.

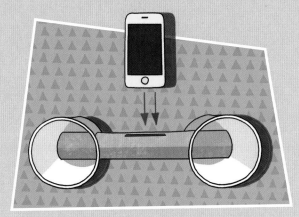

5. Stand the speakers on a table. Start some music playing on the phone, and push it into the hole in the tube.

HOW DOES IT WORK?

When the smartphone plays music, the vibrations spread out in all directions, so they don't sound very loud. When the phone is in the speakers, the vibrations spread into the tube, and then into the paper cups and the air inside them. This collects the sound and makes it point in one direction, so it sounds louder.

WHY DO BALLOONS POP?

Balloons are fun, but sooner or later they POP! What makes that loud popping noise, and why? Banish nervous people to a different room for this loud experiment!

WHAT YOU'LL NEED:

* ✹ Several balloons
* ✹ A candle and candle holder
* ✹ Matches
* ✹ Paper
* ✹ Scissors
* ✹ A pin for popping!

⚠ ASK AN ADULT!

1.
Blow up your balloons and tie them closed. Keep them in a safe place away from your experiment area.

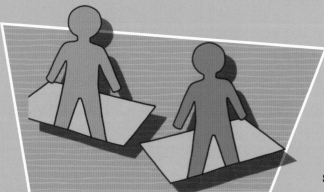

2.
Cut some little figures out of your paper, with rectangles at the bottom, like this. Fold the rectangles flat so your figures will stand up.

3.

Hold a balloon about 6 inches (15cm) away from your paper figures, and pop the balloon with a pin. What happens to the people?

4.

Ask an adult to put your candle in its holder and light it with a match. Again, hold a balloon 6 inches (15cm) away and pop it with a pin. What happens to the candle?

HOW DOES IT WORK?

When you blow up a balloon, you fill it with lots of air. The air is under a lot of pressure—it's tightly squashed inside the balloon. When you pop a balloon, the squashed air suddenly escapes. It rushes outward at high speed. This makes a strong ripple in the air, called a pressure wave. It hits your ears as a loud bang and can also blow out a candle or blow over a paper figure.

Explosions cause a pressure wave too. That's why when there's an explosion, the things around it can get blown apart or blown away.

MESSY EXPERIMENTS

As every scientist knows, some experiments are messier than others. The experiments in this chapter involve gloopy slime, confeti, messy explosions, or just getting soaking wet. Get your old clothes on!

MESSY SCIENCE
So what type of experiments make the most mess, and why?

Chemical reactions
A chemical reaction happens when two different chemicals or substances mix together and react, or change. Not all chemicals react together, but when they do, it can certainly be messy.

Messy materials
Experimenting with water, oil, eggs, paint, or other messy stuff is never going to be neat and tidy.

Explosions
Crazy explosions shoot everything in all directions. There are many ways to create an explosion, and you'll find a few in the following pages.

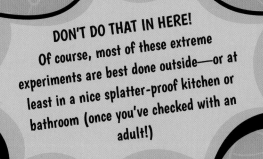

DON'T DO THAT IN HERE!
Of course, most of these extreme experiments are best done outside—or at least in a nice splatter-proof kitchen or bathroom (once you've checked with an adult!)

Make a mini mess

For starters, try this simple experiment to see a basic chemical reaction at work. (Hold on to the ingredients, as you'll be needing them again soon.)

You'll need white vinegar and baking soda (also called bicarbonate of soda)—both available in a supermarket.

Put a small cup or glass in a bowl, and add some vinegar to the cup or glass until it's about half full. Then get a heaped teaspoon of baking soda, and drop it in the vinegar. What happens?

HOW DOES IT WORK?

In a chemical reaction, chemicals combine and change to make new chemicals. In this experiment, the vinegar and the baking soda react to make a gas called carbon dioxide. The gas makes lots of bubbles that make the mixture foam up. The reaction also makes other chemicals. Luckily for you, they're harmless! But some reactions aren't so safe. Sometimes they can create dangerous chemicals, explosions, or flames. So always follow the instructions carefully, and don't mix the wrong things together!

THE EXPLODING BAG

This experiment reveals the true power of a chemical reaction taking place inside a plastic bag. Stand well back!

WHAT YOU'LL NEED:

* White vinegar
* Baking soda (sometimes known as bicarbonate of soda)
* Warm water
* A tablespoon
* A measuring cup or average-sized drinking cup
* A plastic food or freezer bag
* A piece of kitchen roll or tissue
* A big outdoor space

1. Lay the piece of kitchen paper or tissue flat and put 2 tablespoons of baking soda into the middle.

Some food bags have a seal that you can press tightly closed. If you don't have this type, use a large sandwich bag and tie a tight knot in it instead.

2. Fold the paper up so that the powder is held safely inside, like this.

3. Put about a quarter of a cup of warm water into the bag. Then add about half a cup of vinegar. Hold the bag upright so that the liquid doesn't spill out.

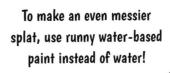
This is easier with two people—one to hold the paper up, the other to close the bag.

HOW DOES IT WORK?

The vinegar and baking soda react and make carbon dioxide gas (the warm water helps to speed things up). As more and more gas is made, it fills up the bag and tries to escape. Finally, the bag can't hold it in any more, and ... SPLAT!

4. Go outside, if you aren't there already. Now put the folded-up paper inside the bag, but keep it away from the liquid. Seal or tie up the bag tightly so no air can escape.

5. Once the bag is sealed shut, let the paper parcel drop into the liquid. Put the bag down on the ground and wait to see what happens!

To make an even messier splat, use runny water-based paint instead of water!

FIZZ FOUNTAIN

This famous experiment makes messy foaming cola splurt all over the place. Some versions of this experiment use candy, but salt works even better!

WHAT YOU'LL NEED:
* A big bottle of diet cola
* A bag of salt
* A piece of paper
* An outdoor space

Don't keep the cola in the fridge—it works better if it's at room temperature.

1. Open the cola and stand it in a safe place, outdoors and away from anything that you don't want to get messy.

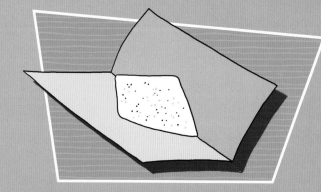

2. Fold your piece of paper in half and pour salt into the fold. Use as much salt as you can comfortably hold in the paper.

3. Line up the end of the fold with the top of the bottle, then carefully tip the salt into the cola, so that it slides in quickly.

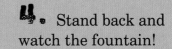

4. Stand back and watch the fountain!

HOW DOES IT WORK?

Fizzy drinks contain a lot of carbon dioxide gas, which is dissolved in the liquid. Normally, the bubbles of gas come out of the drink gradually. But the salt makes it come out much faster. Scientists think this is because the rough surfaces of the salt granules give the gas something to stick to, and it forms large bubbles. Suddenly, there's so much gas that it can't fit in the bottle, so the foamy cola shoots out.

Don't worry about having cola and salt in the same meal. An explosion only happens when a lot of salt and cola are mixed together very quickly (cola with chips might make you burp, though).

HOMEMADE LAVA LAMP

A lava lamp makes bubbles of colorful hot wax float up and down inside a glass bottle. You can make your own simple version with oil, water, and food coloring.

WHAT YOU'LL NEED:

* A tall, clear container, such as a glass jar or bottle
* A bottle of sunflower oil (the type used for cooking)
* Warm water
* Liquid food coloring
* Baking powder
* A spoon

If you don't have baking powder, you could use a fizzing bath bomb broken into small pieces, or a fizzy anti-indigestion drink tablet.

1. First, pour some warm water into your glass container, until it's about a quarter full. Add a few drops of food coloring in your favorite color.

2. Carefully pour in sunflower oil until the container is about three-quarters full. The liquids will swirl about so give them a few moments to settle.

3. Now take a spoonful of baking powder and drop it into the container. If it sits on top of the oil at first, push it down with the spoon.

4. Watch the container from the side to see what happens.

HOW DOES IT WORK?
The baking powder contains chemicals that react with the water to make gas bubbles. The water is heavier than the oil, so the oil floats on top of it. But the bubbles are lighter, so they float to get to the top of the oil. They slowly force their way up through the oil, taking some of the colored water with them.

STREAM OF LIGHT

Light always travels in straight lines ... or does it? In this experiment you can make a beam of light travel along a curved stream of water.

WHAT YOU'LL NEED:
* A large, clear, plastic drinks bottle
* Sharp, pointy scissors
* Water
* A large bucket, sink, or bathtub to catch the water
* A bright flashlight or laser pointer

⚠ ASK AN ADULT!

1. Ask an adult to make a small hole, about ¼ inch (0.5cm) across, near the bottom of the bottle. They can do this by carefully sticking the pointed tip of the scissors in and twisting it around.

2. Cover the hole with a finger, and fill the bottle to the brim with water. Stand the bottle on a flat surface next to the bucket, sink, or bathtub, with the hole facing it.

Get a friend to help you with this step.

3. Turn off the lights in the room so that you can see the flashlight light better. Switch on the flashlight or laser pointer and shine it from behind the bottle, through the water inside, and toward the hole.

HOW DOES IT WORK?
Light does travel in straight lines, but it also bounces, or reflects, off shiny surfaces. When light enters the water stream, it reflects off the inside surface of the water. It bounces to and fro inside the water stream, following its path.

4. Remove the finger and let the water flow out. You should see light flowing along the stream of water. Put your hand under it to see if it makes a spot of light on your skin.

This is the science behind fiber-optic technology, which carries light along tiny glass tubes. As light moves so fast, fiber-optic cables can be used to carry lots of information in the form of light signals. They're often used as internet cables.

SLO-MO WATER BALL

What would happen if you popped a balloon full of water on the International Space Station? This experiment might give you some idea!

WHAT YOU'LL NEED:

* A balloon
* Water
* String
* Something to hang the balloon from, such as a low tree-branch or washing line
* A pin
* A smartphone or digital camera with a slow-motion filming option

1. Blow the balloon up to stretch it, then let it go down. To fill it with water, stretch the neck of the balloon over a faucet, and run the faucet slowly. You only need to fill the balloon to about half the usual size.

2. Tie the balloon closed, and tie some string around the knot. Hang the balloon up somewhere outdoors, away from anything you don't want to get wet!

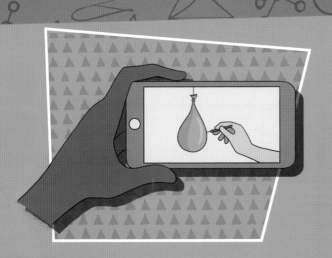

3. Ask a friend to film the balloon on a slow-motion setting while you pop it (or you could set up the camera to do this by itself, using a tripod). Don't let your phone or camera get wet.

4. Once the camera is running, take the pin and gently pop the balloon. You need to do it gently so that the balloon stays as still as possible. Then play back what happened!

HOW DOES IT WORK?

Thanks to Earth's gravity, when you pop the balloon the water will soon splat all over the ground. But when you view it in slow motion, you'll see that the popped balloon shrinks away very fast, before the water has a chance to start falling. For a moment, a perfect balloon-shaped ball of water hangs in mid-air.

Astronauts have actually popped balloons full of water on the International Space Station. You could ask an adult to help you find a video of this on the internet.

CONFETTI CANNON

This simple shooter made from a balloon and a cup will fire a huge burst of confetti into the air. Perfect for parties! (As long as you don't mind a massive mess, that is ...)

WHAT YOU'LL NEED:

* ✹ A paper cup
* ✹ A balloon
* ✹ Scissors or a craft knife
* ✹ Clear tape
* ✹ Confetti
* ⚠ ASK AN ADULT!

1. Ask an adult to cut out the bottom of the paper cup using a craft knife or sharp scissors.

You can buy confetti at craft and stationery stores—or make your own by cutting colored paper or tissue paper into little pieces. You can also use a hole punch to make lots of holes in colored paper, then collect all the tiny circles that fall out.

2. Cut the round end off a balloon, and tie a knot in the neck end. Then stretch it over the bottom of your paper cup, and sticky tape it firmly in place.

3. Now pour your confetti into the cup—and keep it somewhere safe until the moment comes to fire it!

What else could you put in your cannon? Anything small and light will work—try sequins or mini craft pom-poms.

4. When you're ready, hold the cup in one hand, and pull back the balloon with the other.

5. Then 3 ... 2 ... 1 ... let go! Confetti should be flying through the air.

HOW DOES IT WORK?

The balloon skin is elastic and stretchy, like a rubber band. When you pull it down, it stretches, and this stores up energy. When you let go, all this energy is released at once. The balloon skin springs back up at high speed, pushing the confetti out with a bang!

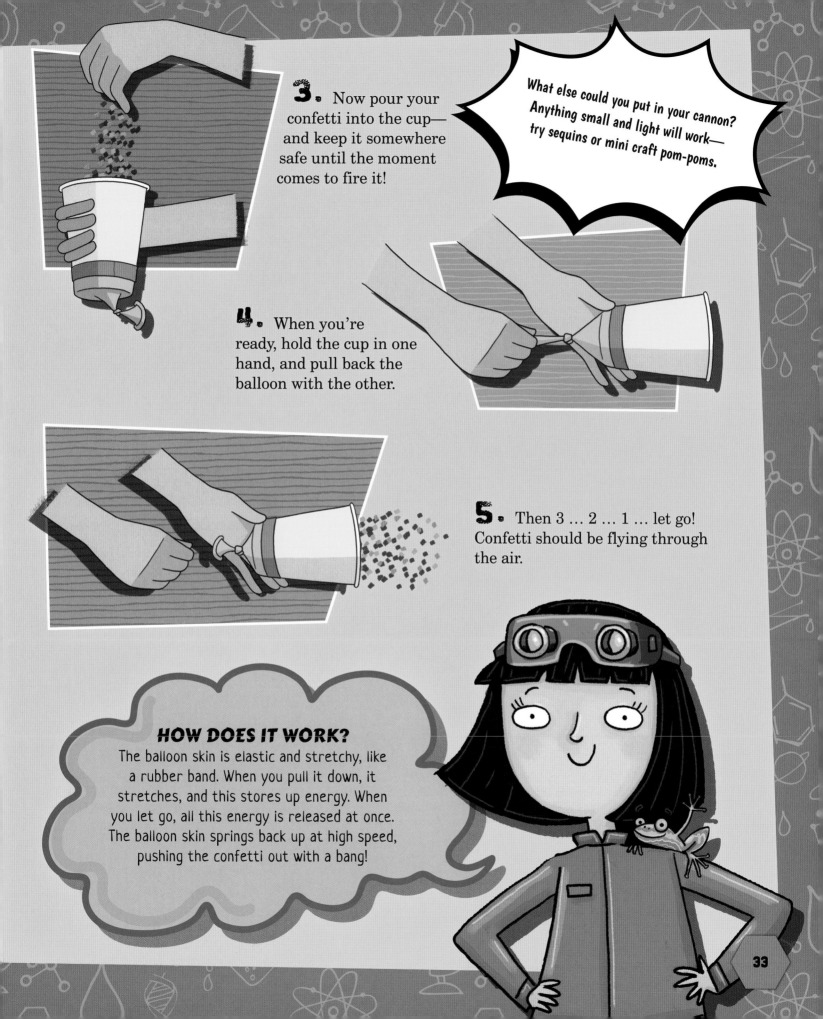

33

ODD OOBLECK

This strange substance is named after the green slime in a book by the famous writer, Dr. Seuss. It's easy to make, but behaves in some very odd ways ...

WHAT YOU'LL NEED:

* One or more packets of cornstarch (also called cornflour)
* Water
* A measuring pitcher
* A large, shallow, plastic food container or mixing bowl
* Green food coloring (optional)
* Old clothes and newspaper

1. Carefully pour your cornstarch into the measuring pitcher to check how much you have. Then tip the cornstarch into the container.

Oobleck is nontoxic, but messy—REALLY messy. Do this experiment in a kitchen or bathroom, and spread out newspapers to protect the surroundings. Or you could do it outdoors.

2. Measure out half as much water as you have cornstarch. For example, if you have 2 cups (600ml) of cornstarch, measure 1 cup (300ml) of water. Add a few drops of food coloring if you like.

3. Add some of the water to the cornstarch and mix it with your hands (this can take a while). Add more water, bit by bit, until you have a gloopy, slimy mixture.

4. Now try these tests to see what the mixture does.

- Grab a handful of oobleck and squeeze it tight. Then let go and open your hands out.
- Pour out a puddle of oobleck, then try to push your fingers through it quickly.

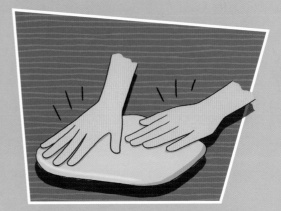

- Let a plastic toy figure sink into the oobleck as if it was quicksand, then try to pull it out quickly.

- Press your hand slowly into the oobleck—then try hitting it hard. What happens?

HOW DOES IT WORK?
Oobleck can behave like a solid or a liquid. When it's pressed hard, the ingredients lock together and it acts like a solid. But when it's handled gently, it flows like a liquid. In bigger and even messier experiments, people have filled swimming pools with oobleck and managed to run over the surface!

MYSTERIOUS EXPERIMENTS

Science can behave in some VERY strange ways. This section is full of experiments that make you go "Wow! How does that work!?" and "Wait—WHAT just happened!?" They're great for amazing your friends and family.

WHY IS SCIENCE SURPRISING?

Most of the time, our brains make good predictions about how objects and materials will behave, based on our past experiences. However, sometimes an experiment can make something behave in an unexpected way—it might even seem impossible! It's breaking the rules our brains have learned, but it's not breaking the rules of science. That's what will make you gasp!

Mysterious science

None of these things are magical—they all happen according to the rules of science. But the more you learn about science, the more you find out that it really IS quite bizarre. For instance, did you know that ...

A particle (tiny bit of matter) can actually be in two places at once.

Time can slow down if you're moving fast enough!

At very low temperatures, helium can flow against gravity.

Mobius madness

Let the weirdness begin with this fun mini experiment!

You need a strip of thin cardboard, about 1 inch (3cm) wide and 12 inches (30cm) long. Bring the ends together to make a loop, but before joining them together, flip one end over so that there's a twist in the strip. Then tape the ends together. The twisted strip is called a Mobius strip.

Take a pair of scissors with a pointy tip, and cut into the middle of the strip. Ask an adult to help if it's tricky.
Cut all the way along the middle until you get back to where you started.

You've cut the strip in half, right ...

... OR HAVE YOU???

HOW DOES IT WORK?

When you twist the end over, you join one edge of the strip to the other edge. Instead of two edges, it now has one long continuous edge. You can't cut it in two because one side is continuous with the other. Simple, isn't it?

AMAZIN' RAISIN

What do you mean, you've never dropped a raisin into your soda? You just have to try it! There's mysterious science at work.

WHAT YOU'LL NEED:
* A new bottle of colorless soda (such as Sprite® or 7 Up®)
* A tall, clear glass
* Raisins

This will work with most sodas, but clear ones make it easier for you to see what the raisins are up to.

1. Open the bottle and pour soda into the glass, filling it almost to the top. Wait for the bubbles to settle down (don't shake the bottle first!).

2. Take a few raisins (large ones works best) and gently drop them into the glass. Watch what they do. Give it a few minutes—it may take a little while to see what's happening.

3. If it works, your raisins will start to behave strangely. They'll sink to the bottom, wait there for a bit, then float up to the surface. After hanging around there for a while, they'll head back to the bottom—and repeat!

HOW DOES IT WORK?

The soda has carbon dioxide gas dissolved in it—this is what makes the bubbles. The rough, crinkly surface of the raisins helps carbon dioxide bubbles come out of the liquid and stick to the raisins. When a raisin has enough bubbles stuck to it, they make it lighter, and up it floats. But when it reaches the surface, some of the bubbles pop. The raisin is now heavier again, and sinks. And so on ...

You can try this with other objects, too. What happens if you use a berry, a jelly bean, or a bit of chocolate instead of a raisin? What works best?

SUGAR LIGHTS

Where does light come from? The Sun, the stars, lightbulbs, flashlights, candles, and glow sticks, of course. You've probably heard of fireflies and deep-sea fish that can light up, too. Oh, and sugar lumps!

WHAT YOU'LL NEED:

* ✹ Sugar lumps
* ✹ Hard, sugary candies, such as mints
* ✹ A plastic sandwich bag (self-sealing if possible)
* ✹ Pliers
* ✹ A very dark place

(!) ASK AN ADULT!

1. Put a few sugar lumps and candies into the sandwich bag, and seal it up or tie it closed. This is to make sure you don't spill sugar everywhere.

2. Go into your dark place. It could be a dark room at night, or just make a dark den under a blanket.

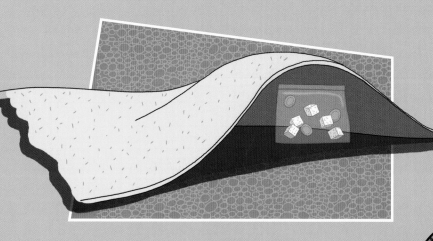

3. Ask an adult to use the pliers, as they can nip your fingers. In the dark, get the adult to hold the pliers around a candy or sugar lump (through the bag, with the sugar and candies inside).

4. Watch carefully as the adult squeezes the pliers to crush the candy or sugar lump as fast as possible. If it's dark enough, you should see a glow of light.

HOW DOES IT WORK?

This strange light is called triboluminescence. It's made by some materials when they are crushed, squeezed, or ripped apart. Scientists aren't really sure why!

There are more ways to make triboluminescence. **TRY THESE!**

- Rip open a self-seal envelope.
- Stick two strips of clear tape or packing tape together, then rip them apart as fast as possible.
- Get two rose quartz crystals and rub them together.
- Ask an adult to put some sugar lumps in a food processor, and blend them.

THE BOUNCY EGG

Take a perfectly normal, raw egg, and turn it into a bouncy rubber ball (well, an egg-shaped ball!) with this bizarre experiment.

WHAT YOU'LL NEED:

* A raw egg
* White vinegar
* A small jar or food container (big enough for the egg) with a lid
* A larger container or bowl
* A plate

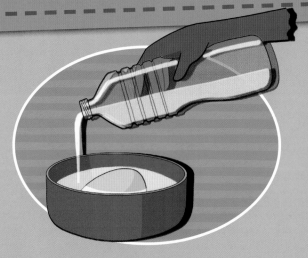

1. Take your egg and gently put it into the small container. Pour in white vinegar until it completely covers the egg. Put the lid on and press or screw it down firmly.

The large container is to catch any vinegar that may leak out, as it's pretty smelly.

2. Now take the container with the egg inside, and put in into the larger container or bowl. Leave your egg to soak for at least 24 hours. You can look at it every so often to see what it's doing, but avoid picking it up or poking it.

HOW DOES IT WORK?

An egg's shell contains a material called calcium carbonate, which makes it hard. Vinegar reacts with calcium carbonate and makes it dissolve away, leaving the inner part, which is a stretchy skin or "membrane." It can still hold the raw egg in, though it's not as strong—and it can bounce.

3. When the time is up, take off the lid and carefully take the egg out. It will have strange bits of "skin" on it—gently wash them off under a tap.

4. The egg should feel strangely soft and rubbery. Drop it onto the plate from a few inches up in the air, and it should bounce!

Do this really carefully, as the egg inside is still raw, and it may splat open. The person who splats it has to clean it up!

FLOWERS AND STARS

Make the flowers bloom and the stars come out with this simple paper experiment. All you need to make it work is water.

WHAT YOU'LL NEED:
* Paper
* Colored pencils or crayons
* Scissors
* A large, shallow plate or container

1. Draw flower and star shapes on the paper. They should each have a circle in the middle, and petals or points around the edge, like these ones.

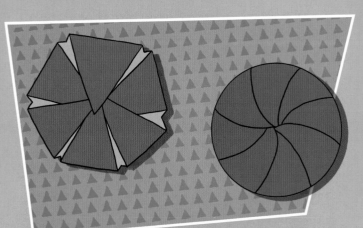

2. Cut out your flower and star shapes, and, if you like, decorate and color them in. Then fold all the petals or points inward, so that they cover the middle.

3. Put your container or plate on a flat surface, and fill it with water almost to the top. Now drop your stars and flowers in, folded side upward.

You can take the flowers and stars out, leave them to dry, and use them over and over again.

HOW DOES IT WORK?

Paper is a porous substance, which means it is full of tiny spaces that can soak up water. As water soaks into the paper, it makes it swell and get thicker. When the paper is thicker, it's hard for the folds to stay shut, and they quickly get pushed open.

For a fancier version, make one larger star or flower, and one smaller one. Stick the smaller one inside the bigger one, and fold them both up. The larger, outside one will open first, and the inside one will open more slowly, as it takes longer for the water to reach it.

EGG IN A BOTTLE

This experiment is great for amazing a crowd of people. They'll get to see an egg being sucked right inside a glass bottle by the sheer power of science.

WHAT YOU'LL NEED:

★ A glass bottle with a wide opening, about 1½ inches (3cm) across

★ An egg that's just slightly wider than the opening of your bottle

★ A pan

★ A stove

★ A sink

★ Cooking oil

★ Matches

⚠ ASK AN ADULT!

1. Ask an adult to hard-boil your egg by boiling it in a pan of water for 10 minutes, then cool it in cold water. When it's cool, carefully peel off the shell, and rinse the egg.

The type of wide-topped bottle you need is sometimes used for juice, iced tea, or chopped tomatoes. An old-fashioned glass milk bottle will also work well.

2. Make sure your glass bottle is clean and dry. Use your finger to smear a little cooking oil around the neck and top of the bottle.

3. Sit the egg in the top of the bottle to check that it is too big to fall in. Then put it to one side, within easy reach (if it does fall in, take it out and try again with a larger egg).

For the egg, if you get a "mixed sizes" box of eggs, you should find one that's just right.

4. Ask an adult to light a match, wait a second or two, then drop it into the bottle. Quickly put the egg on top of the bottle, and it should start being pulled down inside.

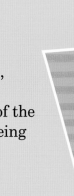

5. It should take just a couple of seconds for the egg to be completely sucked inside the bottle.

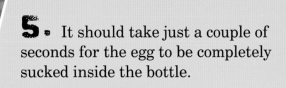

HOW DOES IT WORK?

Air expands as it gets hotter, and shrinks as it gets cooler. The flame heats up the air in the bottle, making it expand. With the egg on top, the match goes out, and the air starts to cool and shrink, reducing the pressure in the bottle. The air pressure on the outside is higher, so it pushes down on the egg, and forces it inside.

INVISIBLE SNUFFER

With this experiment, you can put out a candle flame without touching it or blowing it. Instead, it gets snuffed out by a mysterious stream of something invisible!

WHAT YOU'LL NEED:

* ✸ A small pitcher
* ✸ White vinegar
* ✸ Baking soda (sometimes known as bicarbonate of soda)
* ✸ A teaspoon
* ✸ A candle, holder, and matches

⚠ ASK AN ADULT!

1. First, ask an adult to put the candle in its holder, and light it with a match. Stand it somewhere safe, and put the pitcher near to it, but not too close—about 12 inches (30cm) away.

2. Pour some vinegar into the pitcher until it's about 2 inches (4cm) deep. Then take a heaped teaspoon of baking soda, and stir it into the vinegar. It will foam and bubble.

3. Now ask an adult to quickly pick up the pitcher, and tilt it carefully over the candle, as if pouring water onto the flame. They must tip it only slightly, so that no liquid or foam gets out.

4. If it works, the candle flame will flicker and go out.

HOW DOES IT WORK?

As you've seen with other experiments in this book, when vinegar and baking soda react together, they make a gas, carbon dioxide. Carbon dioxide is heavier than air, which means you can "pour" it out of a jug and it will flow downward. The candle flame needs oxygen from the air to keep burning. But the carbon dioxide gas pushes the air out of the way, so the candle goes out.

Some types of fire extinguishers contain carbon dioxide gas.

MAKE TINY LIGHTNING!

We're not joking ... in this experiment you really can make a flash of lightning, just like the lightning you see in a thunderstorm. The only difference is it's really, really tiny! (And a lot safer ...)

WHAT YOU'LL NEED:
* A balloon
* A metal spoon
* A completely dark room

1. First, get your room ready. Unless it has no windows, it will be easiest to make it really dark when it's also dark outside. Switch off the lights, any screens, and machines with LEDs.

2. Outside the room (so you can see what you're doing), blow up the balloon and tie it. Hold the spoon in one hand and the balloon in the other. Now rub the balloon on your hair, quite fast, for a long time—at least a minute.

Yes, you'll get super-messy hair. Sorry about that!

3. Keeping the balloon and the spoon apart, and not touching anything, go into the dark room (getting someone else to close the door for you).

HOW DOES IT WORK?

The rubbing makes tiny things called electrons come off your hair and onto the balloon. These extra electrons build up and give the balloon an electric charge, called static electricity. When the spoon comes near the balloon, the electrons jump across the gap as a spark of electricity.

4. Now hold the balloon up in front of you, and slowly move the spoon toward it. If you've rubbed the balloon enough, a mini lightning spark will zap across the gap!

HOT AND COLD EXPERIMENTS

Heat and cold affect us humans all the time, as we feel them through our skin. In fact, heat and cold have a big effect on everything else, too. Try these experiments to see how!

What is heat?

To us, heat feels pleasantly warm, or painfully scorching, while cold feels cooling, or bitterly sharp. But our experience of heat and cold are caused by just one simple thing—movement.

All matter—the stuff that everything is made of—is made up of tiny atoms, or groups of atoms called molecules. Whether they're in a solid, a liquid, or a gas, they are always moving.

When things get hotter, their atoms and molecules get more energy, and move faster. The hotter things are, the more the molecules move. Heat is simply made of movement. Cold is the opposite—there's less energy, and less movement.

Heat can spread from one thing to another as the movement is passed on. That's why putting your feet on a cozy hot water bottle warms them up!

Changes of state

Heat and cold can also make things change between a solid, a liquid, and a gas. For example, when puddles get really cold they freeze solid. Washing dries quickly in the sun, as the water turns into water vapor, a gas, and floats away. Chocolate melts from a solid to a liquid in your mouth, or when held in your hand.

Hot air, cold air

Try this simple experiment to see what happens to air as it heats up and cools down. You'll need an empty plastic bottle, a balloon, a bowl of water with ice cubes in it, and a bowl of very hot water (ask an adult to get this ready for you.)

First, blow up the balloon and let it go down, then stretch it over the top of the bottle. Stand the bottle in the hot water, and hold it there for a few minutes. What happens?

Then move the bottle to the bowl with ice in it, and hold it there. What does the balloon do now?

HOW DOES IT WORK?

The bottle is full of air, which is made of gas. The air's molecules are always zooming around and crashing into each other. When the hot water heats the air, the molecules speed up. They push against each other more, and this makes them spread out and take up more space. So the air expands (gets bigger) and starts to inflate the balloon.

WATCH OUT!

These extreme experiments involve candles, hot water, hot ovens, and freezing ice. Take care when you're experimenting, and have an adult handy to do anything that involves a lot of heat.

HYDROTHERMAL VENT

At the bottom of deep oceans, there are hydrothermal vents, where hot water full of dissolved minerals comes shooting out from under the sea bed. This experiment has the same effect—but how?

WHAT YOU'LL NEED:
* ✷ A small empty glass bottle, such as a food coloring bottle
* ✷ String
* ✷ Scissors
* ✷ Hot and cold water
* ✷ Liquid food coloring
* ✷ A large plastic container or bowl
* ✷ A pitcher

⚠ ASK AN ADULT!

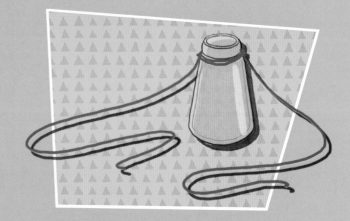

1. Cut a piece of string about 2 feet (50cm) long. Tie the middle of the string around the neck of the bottle, leaving the two long ends free.

2. Stand your large bowl or container on a table, and use the pitcher to fill it with cold water.

3. Add few drops of food coloring to the small bottle. Then ask an adult to fill it with hot water, almost to the brim.

HOW DOES IT WORK?

Like air, water expands and spreads out when it's hotter, becoming less dense. Density means how heavy or light something is for its size. The hot water is lighter than the cold water around it, so it floats up to the top of the bowl, while the colder water sinks. The food coloring lets you see this happening.

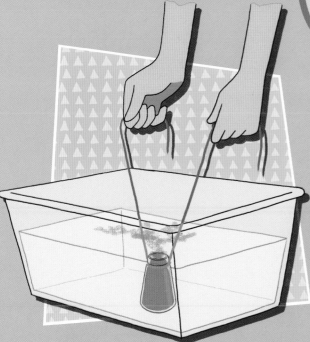

4. Hold the string handles and quickly lower the bottle into the container or bowl of cold water, so that it stands on the bottom. What happens?

SPEED IT UP!

Want your chemical reaction to go faster? Just make it hotter! This simple experiment is a great demonstration of how heat speeds up reactions.

WHAT YOU'LL NEED:

* ✸ Two tall, narrow glasses or jars
* ✸ A tray
* ✸ Two small bowls or cups
* ✸ Baking soda (sometimes known as bicarbonate of soda)
* ✸ White vinegar
* ✸ A teaspoon
* ✸ A tablespoon
* ✸ Hot and cold water

(!) ASK AN ADULT!

1. Stand your two tall glasses on the tray, side by side. Carefully measure three level teaspoons of baking soda into each glass. The amounts must be exactly the same.

Make a "level" spoonful by filling the spoon, then scraping off the top with a knife so that the powder lies flat.

2. Take your two bowls, and measure out two tablespoons of vinegar into each. Then add two tablespoons of cold water to one of the bowls.

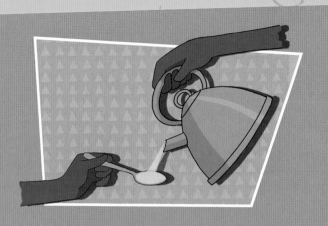

3. Ask an adult to add two tablespoons of very hot water to the other bowl.

4. Quickly take both the bowls of liquid, and, at the same moment, pour them into the two glasses. Watch them carefully! The tray should catch any mess (hopefully).

HOW DOES IT WORK?

If it works, the reaction in the glass with the hot water will be much faster. This is because of the way heat makes atoms and molecules zoom around more quickly. In the hot water and vinegar mixture, the particles are moving faster, so they crash into and react with the baking soda much more rapidly.

Scientists often add heat to reactions to speed them up.

UNDERWATER CANDLE

Can a candle really burn underwater? Well ... kind of! This experiment uses both heat and cold to give a candle flame an underwater home.

WHAT YOU'LL NEED:

* A cylinder-shaped pillar candle
* A large glass or metal bowl that's deeper than the candle
* Poster putty
* A pitcher
* Matches
* Water

⚠ ASK AN ADULT!

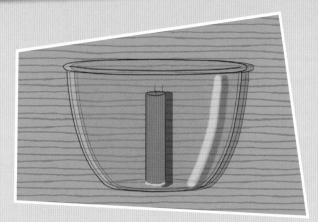

1. Roll a ball of poster putty about ½ inch (2cm) across, and stick it to the base of the candle. Press the candle hard into the bottom of the bowl, so that it stands upright and stays in place.

2. Stand the bowl somewhere safe and well away from other objects. Use the pitcher to fill the bowl with cold water, until the water level is about ¼ inch (1cm) below the candle's wick.

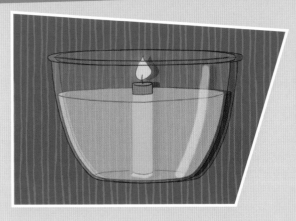

3. Once the water is calm, ask the adult to light the candle. Leave it burning, but make sure there is always an adult in the room to keep an eye on it.

4. The candle will start to burn down. But instead of going out, the flame should get lower and lower, inside a wall of wax that keeps the water out.

How far below the water level will it go? Can you take a photo from the side, showing the flame rising out of the water?

HOW DOES IT WORK?

When you light a candle, it starts burning down, using up the wax. The heat usually melts some of the wax, too, and it drips down the sides. In the water, the sides of the candle don't melt so much, because the water around them is keeping them cool. Only the wax in the middle burns down, so the flame gets lower and lower—until it's under the water surface!

PEA AND SPOON RACE

Not an egg and spoon race, but a pea and spoon race! But you don't have to run anywhere—in this experiment, heat is trying to win the race.

WHAT YOU'LL NEED:

* ✹ Three spoons—one wooden, one metal, and one plastic, as similar in size and shape as possible.
* ✹ Three peas, all the same size (not frozen)
* ✹ Soft butter
* ✹ A heatproof glass or coffee mug
* ✹ Very hot water

* ⚠ ASK AN ADULT!

1. First, make sure your spoons are clean, dry, and cold, not warm.

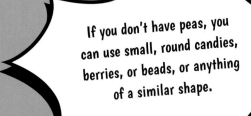

If you don't have peas, you can use small, round candies, berries, or beads, or anything of a similar shape.

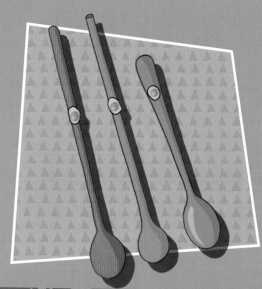

2. Use a dab of butter to stick a pea to each spoon handle. If the spoons are different lengths, line them up, and put the pea the same distance away from the round end on each one, like this.

3. Ask an adult to half-fill the glass with hot water. Stand all three spoons in the water, all at the same time. Make them lean away so that their handles are not directly above the water.

4. The race is on! Heat will spread up from the water through the spoon handles. When each spoon handle gets warm, the butter will melt, and the pea will drop off. Which do you think will be first?

HOW DOES IT WORK?

When heat spreads through an object, it's called heat conduction. Some materials are much better at conducting heat than others. For example, metals are good conductors, and heat spreads through them quickly. Wood and plastic don't conduct heat as well.

Heat conduction is one reason we use different materials for different jobs. For example, a pan is made of metal to conduct heat to the food inside, but the handle may be wooden or plastic, so that it doesn't get too hot to touch.

HEATPROOF BALLOON

Can you hold a balloon in a candle flame without it popping? Of course not! Well, actually, you can, with this extreme experiment.

WHAT YOU'LL NEED:

* Two balloons
* A candle and candle holder
* Matches
* Water

(!) ASK AN ADULT!

Do this experiment in the kitchen or bathroom, just in case it goes wrong and you get water everywhere!

1. First, do a test to check that candles really do make balloons pop. Ask an adult to put the candle in its holder in a safe place, and light it. Blow up the first balloon, tie it closed, and ask the adult to hold it over the candle so that it just touches the flame. Pop!

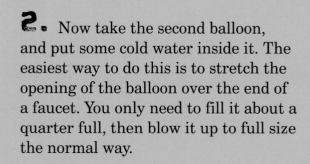

2. Now take the second balloon, and put some cold water inside it. The easiest way to do this is to stretch the opening of the balloon over the end of a faucet. You only need to fill it about a quarter full, then blow it up to full size the normal way.

3. Tie the balloon closed, and dry any water drops off the outside of it. Now ask your adult to carefully hold the balloon over the candle flame, like before.

4. If it works, it should be possible to hold the balloon in the flame for a few seconds, without it popping.

HOW DOES IT WORK?

When the hot flame touches the balloon rubber, it gets so hot that it immediately melts, and the balloon pops. But when there's water in the balloon, the heat from the flame mostly goes into the cold water. It takes a lot of heat energy to warm up water, so it stays cool for a while, and keeps the balloon skin cool, too—even though there's a flame touching it!

GLOSSARY

air pressure The force of air as it pushes on things.

atom A tiny particle that makes up everything in the Universe.

carbon dioxide A gas that can be used to form small bubbles in liquid (such as soda), making it fizzy.

conduction The way that heat spreads through an object.

density A measure of how compact something is and how much matter it is made of.

energy The capacity to move, work, and transfer heat.

expand To increase in size.

force A push or pull on an object that causes a change in its movement.

gas A light, airlike substance that has no fixed shape.

gravity A force that tries to pull two objects together. Earth's gravity is what keeps us on the ground, and what makes objects fall.

inflate To make something bigger by filling it with air.

matter The stuff that makes up you, the world, and everything in the Universe. Matter can be a solid, liquid, or gas.

membrane A thin, flexible layer or covering.

molecule A tiny part of a substance made up of two or more atoms joined together. A molecule is the smallest unit of a substance that still behaves like that substance.

oxygen A gas that is essential for life.

particle A tiny piece of something.

porous Containing many tiny openings through which water can pass.

pressure A force that pushes against something.

solid A substance that has a fixed volume and shape.

water vapor Water in the air in the form of a gas.